Mel Bay Presents

Student's Complete Music Handbook

A Guide to:
  Music Theory
    Music History
      and
        Music Dictionary

By L. Dean Bye

Contents

A Guide to Music Theory

Musical Notation And Pitch

THE STAFF: Music is written on a STAFF consisting of FIVE LINES and FOUR SPACES.

The lines and spaces are numbered upward as shown:

5TH LINE	
4TH LINE	4TH SPACE
3RD LINE	3RD SPACE
2ND LINE	2ND SPACE
1ST LINE	1ST SPACE

THE LINES AND SPACES ARE NAMED AFTER LETTERS OF THE ALPHABET.

THE TREBLE CLEF:

This sign is the treble or G Clef.

The second line of the treble clef is known as the G line. Many people call the treble clef the G clef because it circles around the G line.

The LINES in the Treble Clef are named as follows:

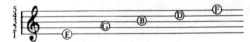

The letters may easily be remembered by the sentence - Every Good Boy Does Fine

The letter - names of the SPACES in the Treble Clef are:

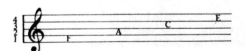

They spell the word F - A - C - E

The Musical Alphabet has <u>seven</u> letters - A B C D E F G

On a separate piece of manuscript paper, practice writing "G" or Treble clef signs.

THE BASE CLEF:

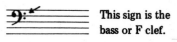

This sign is the bass or F clef.

As we can see, the fourth line of the bass clef is known as the "F" line. Many people call the bass clef the F clef because the two dots are placed on either side of the line. All other letter names are figured from this line.

The Lines on the Bass Clef are named as follows:

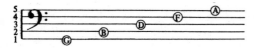

These letters may easily be remembered by the sentence - Good Boys Do Fine Always

The letter - names of the spaces in the Bass Clef are:

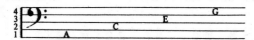

These letters may be remembered by the sentence - All Cars Eat Gas

Ledger lines are short lines placed above and below the staff. Some examples are:

On a separate sheet of Manuscript Paper, practice writing "F" or Bass Clef Signs.

5

When both the treble and bass clefs are combined with an added ledger line (middle C), it is known as the grand staff.

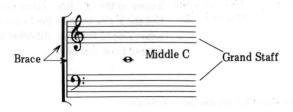

The perpendicular line and the bracket that joins two or more different staves is called a <u>brace.</u>

Staff Notation And Keyboard Position:

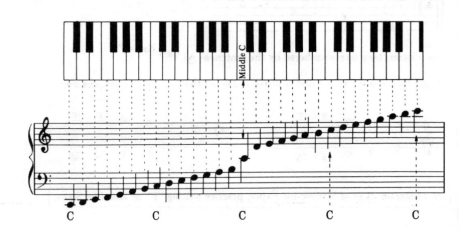

Duration Of Notes And Rests--Meter

TONE:
> A TONE has four characteristics . . . PITCH , DURATION, DYNAMICS and TIMBRE.
>> PITCH: The highness or lowness of a tone.
>> DURATION: The length of a tone.
>> DYNAMICS: The force or power of a tone. (Loudness or softness.).
>> TIMBRE: Quality of the tone.
> A NOTE represents the PITCH AND DURATION of a tone.

NOTES:
> This is a note:

> A note has three parts. They are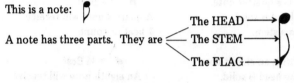

> Notes may be placed in the staff; Above the staff;

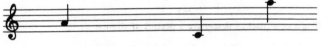

> And below the staff.

> A note will bear the name of the line or space it occupies on the staff. The location of a note in, above or below the staff will indicate the Pitch.

> PITCH: The height or depth of a tone.

> TONE: A musical sound.

REMEMBER: A Note represents the Pitch and Duration of a tone and it will bear the name of the line or space it occupies on the staff.

7

TYPES OF NOTES:

THE TYPE OF NOTE WILL INDICATE THE LENGTH OF ITS SOUND.

○ This is a whole note.
The head is hollow.
It does not have a stem.

○ = 4 Beats
A whole note will receive
4 beats or counts.

♩ This is a half note.
The head is hollow.
It has a stem.

♩ = 2 Beats
A half note will receive
2 beats or counts.

♩ This is a quarter note.
The head is solid.
It has a stem.

♩ = 1 Beat
A quarter note will receive
1 beat or count.

♪ This is an eighth note.
The head is solid.
It has a stem and a flag.

♪ = ½ Beat
An eighth note will receive
one - half beat or count.
(2 for 1 beat)

RESTS:
A REST is a sign used to designate a period of silence.

This period of silence will be of the same duration of time as the note to which it corresponds.

𝄽 This is an eighth rest.   𝄽 This is a quarter rest.

— This is a half rest. Note that it sits on the line.

— This is a whole rest. Note that it hangs down from the line.

NOTES:

Whole	Half	Quarter	Eighth
○	♩	♩	♪
Whole	Half	Quarter	Eighth
4 Counts	2 Counts	1 Count	2 for Count

RESTS:

—	—	𝄽	𝄽

8

When the head of a note is placed above the third line, the stem is usually drawn downward on the left side of the note. When the head of the note is located below the third line the stem usually goes upward on the right side. Notes on the third line may have stems going either way.

A Dot After A Note (or a rest) increases its value by one-half.
See the following examples.

The STAFF is divided into measures by vertical lines called BARS.

Heavy double bars mark the end of a section or strain of music.*

* A division within a piece or movement is shown by a light double bar.

Note: A measure is the space between two bar lines.

The Time Signature

The above examples are common types of time signatures.

 The top number indicates the number of beats per measure.
The bottom number indicates the type of note receiving one beat.

Example: $\frac{4}{4}$ Beats per measure
A quarter-note receives one beat

Signifies so called "common time" and simply another way of designating $\frac{4}{4}$ time.

The symbol for cut time is ¢ . It means to give each note ½ of its written value. For our purposes all we need remember is that when the time signature ¢ appears, we will count $\frac{2}{2}$ instead of $\frac{4}{4}$ or ¢ .

TEMPO

Tempo is the rate of movement or speed of a piece of music. Tempo is indicated by a word or phrase which is very often in Italian.

Some of the most important of these terms are given in the chart below. They are arranged in order from slowest to fastest.*

BASIC TEMPO MARKINGS

Largo - Very slow and stately.
Largamente - Broadly. Quite slow.
Larghetto - Faster than Largo, but slow.
Grave - Seriously, solemn.
Lento - Slowly (often used temporarily)
Adagio - Slowly, very expressive
Andante - Tranquilly, but moving right along.
Andantino - Generally interpreted as slightly faster than Andante.
Moderato - Moderately. It is usually considered the medium point between the slowest and fastest markings.
Allegretto - Animated, but less than Allegro
Allegro - Lively, animated in movement.
Vivace - More rapidly than Allegro.
Presto - Very fast.
Prestissimo - The fastest tempo used.

*Tempo is measured with a <u>metronome,</u> a mechanical (or electric) device for determining the number of beats to be played at the tempo indicated by the composer. Set the metronome using the various tempo markings from the above list and listen so that a feeling for these may be established. Specific metronome markings may appear also as the following examples show.

m.m. ♩ = 70 Seventy metronome beats per minute; a quarter note receives one beat.

m.m. ♩ = 40 Forty metronome beats per minute; a half note receives one beat.

<u>SYNCOPATION:</u> Special rhythmic effects may be acquired in music by placing special accents (>) or <u>emphasis</u> on different beats or parts of a beat. If a natural accent or strong beat is moved from its normal place to a weak beat, we have syncopation. This could be done a number of ways. Study the following examples for some of them. (The accent marks are to show where syncopation occurs.)

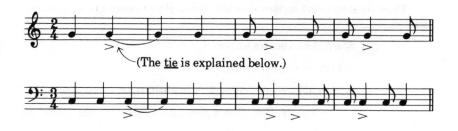

(The <u>tie</u> is explained below.)

THE TIE:

The <u>TIE</u> is a curved line between two notes of the same pitch.
The first note is played and held for the time duration of both.
The second note is not played but held.

Key Signatures– Major/Minor Scales

A <u>half</u> <u>step</u> is the distance from one pitch (tone) to the next nearest pitch (tone) either up or down. This interval is often referred to as a <u>semitone</u>.

Examples: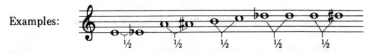

A <u>whole</u> <u>step</u> is two adjacent half steps. This interval is often referred to as a <u>whole</u> <u>tone</u>.

Examples: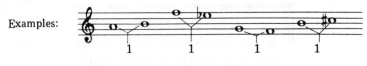

ACCIDENTALS

There are signs called accidentals which, when placed before a note, alter the pitch of the note.

♯ Sharp: raises pitch a half-step

♭ Flat: lowers pitch a half-step

✕ Double-Sharp: raises pitch two half-steps, or one whole-step

♭♭ Double-Flat: lowers pitch two half-steps or one whole-step

♮ Natural: cancels a sharp or a flat

Accidentals affect only the tones within that octave register and within that measure.

> On a separate sheet of manuscript paper, practice writing examples of the above shown accidentals.

Key Signatures

Sharps and flats immediately following the clef sign are called the key signature. These accidentals affect every note on the line or space which they represent throughout the entire composition unless they are cancelled by a natural sign (♮) or a change to another key.

In the following example, every note called F is now raised one half-step to F♯ because a sharp is placed on the F line in the key signature.

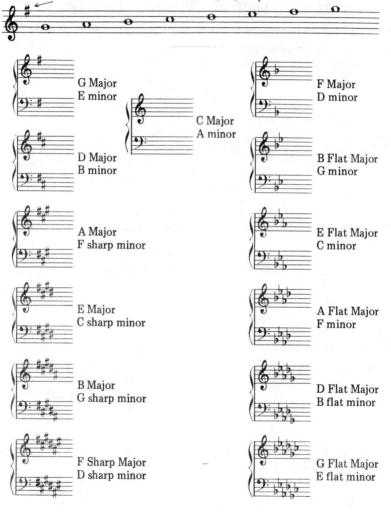

G Major / E minor	F Major / D minor
C Major / A minor	
D Major / B minor	B Flat Major / G minor
A Major / F sharp minor	E Flat Major / C minor
E Major / C sharp minor	A Flat Major / F minor
B Major / G sharp minor	D Flat Major / B flat minor
F Sharp Major / D sharp minor	G Flat Major / E flat minor

> A <u>Diatonic Scale</u> is a series of eight successive notes (the eighth duplicating the first) that are arranged in a systematic relationship of whole and half steps.
>
> The diatonic scale is made up of two types-- <u>Major</u> and <u>Minor</u>.

Building A Major Scale

A major scale is a series of eight notes arranged in this pattern of whole steps and half steps.

C Major
Scale   C D E F G A B C

Root 2nd 3rd 4th 5th 6th 7th Octave
½ STEP   ½ STEP

SCALE TONES		DISTANCE FROM PRECEDING NOTE
ROOT	(C)	
2nd	(D)	Whole Step
3rd	(E)	Whole Step
4th	(F)	½ Step
5th	(G)	Whole Step
6th	(A)	Whole Step
7th	(B)	Whole Step
Octave	(C)	½ Step

WITH THE ABOVE FORMULA YOU
CAN CONSTRUCT ANY MAJOR
   SCALE!

To construct a major scale we first start with the name of the scale (Frequently called the Root or Tonic).

With the C scale this would be the note "C." The rest of the scale would fall in line as follows:

C to D = Whole Step	G to A = Whole Step
D to G = Whole Step	A to B = Whole Step
E to F = ½ Step	B to C = ½ Step
F to G = Whole Step	

G MAJOR SCALE

To construct the G major scale, start with the note G, construct it as follows:

G A B C D E F# G

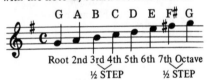

Root 2nd 3rd 4th 5th 6th 7th Octave
½ STEP   ½ STEP

Notice that in order to make our formula work with the G scale we must sharp(#) the F. There must be a whole step between the 6th and 7th tones of the scale. In order to establish a whole step between E and F we must sharp the F.

> Remember: The combination of sharps and flats necessary to form a major scale is called a key signature.
>
> Notice that the order of flats is opposite to the order to sharps.
>
> F# C# G# D# A# E# B#
> Bb Eb Ab Db Gb Cb Fb

Table Of Major Keys And Signatures

C MAJOR has no sharps or flats

G MAJOR has one sharp,	F♯					
D MAJOR has two sharps,	F♯	C♯				
A MAJOR has three sharps,	F♯	C♯	G♯			
E MAJOR has four sharps,	F♯	C♯	G♯	D♯		
B MAJOR has five sharps,	F♯	C♯	G♯	D♯	A♯	
F♯ MAJOR has six sharps,	F♯	C♯	G♯	D♯	A♯	E♯
C♯ MAJOR has seven sharps,	F♯	C♯	G♯	D♯	A♯	E♯	B♯

F MAJOR has one flat,	B♭					
B♭ MAJOR has two flats,	B♭	E♭				
E♭ MAJOR has three flats,	B♭	E♭	A♭			
A♭ MAJOR has four flats,	B♭	E♭	A♭	D♭		
D♭ MAJOR has five flats,	B♭	E♭	A♭	D♭	G♭	
G♭ MAJOR has six flats,	B♭	E♭	A♭	D♭	G♭	C♭
C♭ MAJOR has seven flats,	B♭	E♭	A♭	D♭	G♭	C♭	F♭

The following diagram of the cycle of keys shows the relationship of all the major scales.

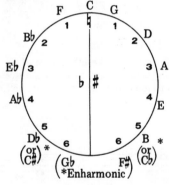

The most important degrees in each key are 1 - 3 - 5 which form the Tonic or I chord of the key.

Write the 1 - 3 - 5 or <u>Tonic</u> of the following keys:
C, G, F, A, E♭, and B.

STARTING WITH C MOVING TO THE RIGHT GIVES US THE KEYS CONTAINING SHARPS AND MOVING TO THE LEFT GIVES US THE KEYS CONTAINING FLATS.

*Enharmonic: Written differently as to notation but sounding the same.

Minor Scales

Each Major key will have a Relative Minor key.
The Relative Minor Scale is built upon the sixth tone of the Major Scale.
The Key Signature of both will be the same.
The Minor Scale will have the same number of tones (7) as the Major.
The difference between the scales is the arrangement of the whole-steps and half-steps.

There are three forms of the minor scale: 1. PURE or NATURAL, 2. HARMONIC, 3. MELODIC.

THE MAJOR AND RELATIVE MINOR KEYS:

D is the 6th Tone of the F
Scale; G is the 6th Tone
of the B Scale, etc.

		C	Am
F	Dm	F♯	D♯m
B♭	Gm	B	G♯m
E♭	Cm	E	C♯m
A♭	Fm	A	F♯m
D♭	B♭m	D	Bm
G♭	E♭m	G	Em

The NATURAL or PURE MINOR SCALE begins on the 6th degree of its relative major scale and ascends or descends for one octave using the key signature of the major scale. We usually use small letters to indicate minor keys. The half steps occur between 2 - 3 and 5 - 6.

c minor (natural)

The HARMONIC MINOR SCALE begins on the 6th degree of its relative major scale and ascends or descends for one octave using the key signature of the major scale except that the 7th tone is raised 1/2 step. (See arrow in the example below) The half steps occur between 2 - 3, and 7 - 8.*

c minor (harmonic)

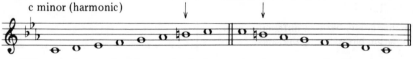

*The raised seventh scale tone in the harmonic minor creates the distance of a step and one half between 6 - 7.

The MELODIC MINOR SCALE also begins on the 6th degree of its relative major scale and ascends or descends for one octave using the key signature of the major scale except that in ascending the 6th and 7th tones are raised 1/2 step and in descending the 6th and 7th tones return to the natural or pure minor scale form.*

c minor (melodic)

*In the melodic minor ascending, the half steps occur between the 2-3 and 7-8 notes

> On a separate sheet of manuscript paper, construct the minor scale for each key and label the Root, Third, and Fifth tones of each scale. Show both the ascending and descending forms of the melodic minor. Finally, write the sharps or flats found in each key signature.

A CHROMATIC SCALE is a scale which consists entirely of half steps. It may be written by the use of accidentals (♯-♭-♮) in connection with the regular key signature. Sharp and natural signs are used for the ascending scale and flat and natural signs for the descending scale.

The filled-in notes designate the ascending and descending chromatic tones in C major in the following example:

> On a separate sheet of manuscript paper, write an ascending chromatic scale in the key of E♭ a and a descending chromatic scale in the key of A. Remember -- frequent drill in any musical skill is <u>necessary</u>.

*Notice that the chromatic scale has a number of <u>enharmonic</u> tones (see page 19). The term enharmonic pertains to tones which are "Spelled" differently but sound the same. For example: a♭-g♯; c♭-b; e♭-d♯; and f♭-e.

Form And Expression Marks

In order to read, write, or understand music, one must know all of the signs, words and abbreviations which are often referred to as the musical vocabulary. Many of these have been given on other pages, but most are included here.

1. A melody is a succession of single tones.

2. A chord is a combination of tones sounded together.

3. A triad is a three note chord.

   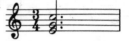

Tones in a melody.   The same tones as a chord.

4. A phrase is a short musical thought - - a musical sentence. The phrase usually finishes on a note of longer duration, or at the end of a rhythmic pattern. A double bar does not necessarily mean the beginning or end of a phrase.

Example:

5. A period is a "complete musical thought" usually made up of two phrases.

Example:

6. A slur is a curved line drawn above or below groups of two or more notes. Usually this means that the notes are to be played or sung legato (Smoothly).

Example:

7. A tie is a curved line connecting two notes of the same letter name and pitch.

Example:

8. When sections or portions of a piece of music are to be repeated, various signs are used.

(A) D.C. (Da Capo) means to repeat from the beginning to the word Fine (the end).

Example: A   *Fine*   B   *D.C.*   (A B A)

(B) D.S. (Dal Segno) means to repeat from the Sign (𝄋) to the word Fine (the end).

Example: A   𝄋   B   *Fine*   C   *D.S.*   (A B C B)

(C) Two dots before a double barline mean to return to the beginning or to another double bar followed by two dots.

Example: A   B   (A A B B)

(D) First and second endings are often used after repetitions in music.

First ending   Second ending
Example: A   1. B   2. C   (A B A C)

9. DYNAMICS are indicated by words such as . . .

Pianissimo	(*pp*)	Very soft
Piano	(*p*)	Soft
Mezzo piano	(*mp*)	Medium soft
Mezzo forte	(*mf*)	Medium loud
Forte	(*f*)	loud
Fortissimo	(*ff*)	Very loud

10. The names of all scale degrees in a diatonic scale are:

First Degree - Tonic
Second Degree - Supertonic
Third Degree - Mediant
Fourth Degree - Subdominant
Fifth Degree - Dominant
Sixth Degree - Submediant
Seventh Degree - Leading Tone
Eighth Degree - Octave

Expression Marks/Abbreviations

ad lib. - giving the performer liberty in matters of tempo and express-ion.

Accel. - Accelerando (increase speed or tempo)

$\overset{>}{\rvert}$ Accent - to stress or to emphasize

Accom. - Accompaniment

a tempo - resume strict time

⟵ A double bar - line
A bar - line

$\lor$, $\,^\text{,}$ - Breath marks

⊕ - Coda

◁ or cresc, - crescendo (get louder)

• - Dot
   1) a dot placed after a note or rest increases the value one half. (Exp. ♩.)
   2) a dot placed below or above a note indicates that the note should be played staccato. (Exp. ♩)

▷ or Dim. - Diminuendo or Decresc. (get softer)

⌢ - a fermata or hold

Fine - the end

♩ (Subdivide) - in this case play four eighth notes.

Leg. - Legato (smoothly and connected)
meno - less
ped. - pedal
piu - more
rall. - rallentando (gradually slower)
repeat - a character indicating that certain measures or passages are to be sung or played twice.
(see previous page)

rit. - ritard or ritardando (gradually slower)

rubato - a flexibility of tempo-a quicken-ing and slowing of the tempo by the performer or conductor.

sforzando (sfz) - a strong accent - imme-diately followed by piano (soft).

♯ ; ♭ ; ♮ - sharp; flat; natural

✗ - Double - Sharp; raises the pitch two half - steps or one whole step.

♭♭ - Double - flat; lowers the pitch two half steps or one whole step.

Sign - a note or character employed in music.

Spiccato - Italian for very detached. (usually used for string instru-ments.)

≡ - a staff

Suspension - the holding of a note in any chord into the chord which follows

♩ or ten. - tenuto - sustain for full value.

Triplet - ♩♩♩ - a group of three notes performed in the time of 2.

Tutti - All - Everyone sings or plays.

Unis. - Unison

Vamp - to improvise an accompaniment

8va. - 8 notes higher

Voce (It.) - the voice

Volume - The power (loudness or softness) of a voice or instrument
Whole step - two half steps or a major second

Intervals And Two-Part Harmony

An <u>interval</u> in music is the distance between two tones with regard to pitch. The interval is counted from the lower note to the upper, including both notes. Intervals remain the same whether we use the bass clef or the treble clef.

Intervals played or written together are called Harmonic.

Intervals played or written one after another are called Melodic.

INTERVALS IN THE SCALE OF C MAJOR

Prime or Unison	Second	Third	Fourth	Fifth	Sixth	Seventh	Octave
Perfect	Major	Major	Perfect	Perfect	Major	Major	Perfect

An Interval is Major when the upper note is found in the major scale of the lower note.

When the distance between two notes of a Major interval is made one half step smaller, it is called a MINOR INTERVAL.

Only SECONDS – THIRDS – SIXTHS – SEVENTHS or Major intervals can be made minor.

Examples:

Major Third   Minor Third   Major Sixth   Minor Sixth   Major Second   Minor Second

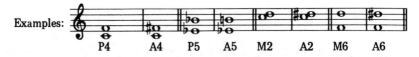

In the minor scales we have PERFECT, MAJOR and MINOR INTERVALS.

If a perfect or a major interval is expanded by a half step it becomes <u>augmented</u>.

Examples:

P4   A4   P5   A5   M2   A2   M6   A6

21

> If a perfect interval is contracted by a half step, it then becomes diminished;
> While if a major interval is contracted a half step, it becomes minor.

Examples: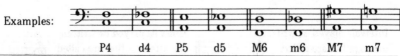

P4   d4   P5   d5   M6   m6   M7   m7

> If a major interval is made minor and then contracted another half step, it
> becomes diminished.

Example:

M3   m3   d3

The four most common Augmented Intervals are as follows:

Maj. 2nd / Aug. 2nd/Per. 4th /Aug. 4th/Per. 5th/Aug. 5th/Maj. 6th/Aug. 6th

The most common Diminished Intervals are shown in the following example:

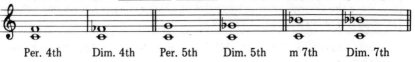

Per. 4th   Dim. 4th   Per. 5th   Dim. 5th   m 7th   Dim. 7th

> Intervals are examples of the simplest harmony used in music. This is often
> called two-part harmony. In its most uncomplicated state a melody would be
> harmonized with a second part written a "third" or a "sixth" lower than the
> melody.

Examples: (The second part is written a "third" lower.)

(The second part is written a "sixth" lower.)

The inversion of an interval is the result of moving one of the tones an octave while the other tone remains stationary. When an interval is inverted, its character is changed.

When intervals are inverted:

1. These changes take place in the interval name.

prime (or unison) becomes octave	fifth becomes fourth
second becomes seventh	sixth becomes third
third becomes sixth	seventh becomes second
fourth becomes fifth	octave becomes prime (or unison)

2. The qualities change as follows:

major becomes minor	diminished becomes augmented
minor becomes major	augmented becomes diminished

3. All qualities are reversed except perfect.

Examples:

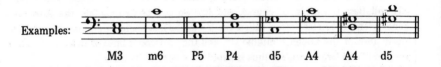

| M3 | m6 | P5 | P4 | d5 | A4 | A4 | d5 |

Remember: Adjustments in an interval may be made with either the top or bottom tone!!

(For more information and drills on Intervals and two-part harmony, see Theory and Harmony for Everyone, published by Mel Bay Publications, Inc.)

Transposition

Transposition is the act of changing music from one key to another key. The most widely used method of transposition is by interval. Very often, the purpose of transposition is to enable a performer to use one system of fingering for a whole family of differently pitched instruments. (In band or orchestral music, for example.) The interval of transposition is measured on the Grand Staff. (See preceding chapter for a discussion of intervals.)

In the following example we will transpose a short phrase from the Key of E♭ Major to the Key of G Major. Because the key of G Major is a third higher than the Key of E♭ Major, we will write each note of the melody a third higher.

All orchestral or band music today is written on one of four clefs. The treble (G) and Bass (F) clefs, of course, and also on one of two C clefs; the Alto and Tenor. The Alto clef (often called the Viola clef), is made by combining the two lower lines of the G clef, "middle C", and the two upper lines of the F clef. This portion of the Grand Staff is thus isolated on a staff of its own.

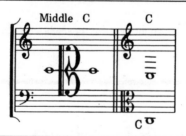

The Tenor Clef is constructed by taking the lowest line of the G clef, "Middle C", and the three upper lines of the F clef. This portion of the Grand Staff is isolated on a staff of its own.

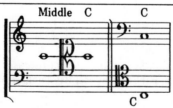

The Tenor Clef is often used by the cello, string bass, trombone, bassoon, and baritone horn.

A transposing instrument is one which sounds a pitch other than the one it reads. Another way to say it would be - it reads pitches other than it sounds. Instruments are very often labelled by the pitch of the scale they sound when they read a "C" scale. A B♭ instrument is one which sounds a B♭ scale when it reads a "C" scale. An E♭ is an instrument which sounds an E♭ scale when it reads a "C" scale. The interval of transposition in measured from "Middle C". Therefore, in order to be able to play "in tune" with the concert pitch, the composer or arranger must transpose some instruments the same interval above or below concert pitch that the instrument sounds above or below that pitch.

The B♭ Soprano instruments include Clarinets, Cornets, Trumpets, and Saxophones. They sound a major second below "Middle C", so they must be written a major second above Middle C".

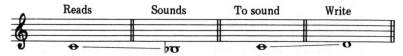

The A soprano instruments include clarinets, cornets, trumpets, and sometimes French horns. They sound a minor third below Middle C, so they must be written a minor third above Middle C.

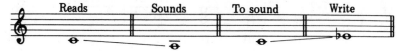

Some additional transposing instruments are as follows:

Instruments	Group Includes:	They sound:	They must be written:
G Alto Instruments	Alto Flute; sometimes French Horn	Perfect fourth below concert pitch	a perfect fourth above concert pitch
F Alto Instruments	French Horn; English Horn; Mellophone; some Saxophones	perfect fifth below concert pitch	a perfect fifth above concert pitch
E♭ Alto Instruments	Alto Saxophones; French Horns; Alto Horns; Mellophones	major sixth below concert pitch	a major sixth above concert pitch
C Tenor Instruments	Bass Flute; Baritone Oboe	octave below written pitch	no transposition necessary

Triads–Chords

A <u>chord</u> consists of two or more tones sounded together. A <u>triad</u> is a chord using three tones.

There are four types of triads: major, minor, augmented, and diminished.

A major chord or triad contains a root, a major third, and a perfect fifth.

The following are
major triads:

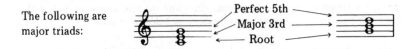

If we build a chord consisting of a root-third-fifth on every degree of a major scale, we will find three major chords.

In the following example, notice the use of ROMAN NUMERALS to help identify the scale degree.

The three major chords occur on the first, I; fourth, IV; and fifth, V, degrees of the major scale.

Each scale degree has a name as well as a number. The first degree, which gives the tone of the key, is called the <u>Tonic.</u> The fifth degree is the "dominating" note of the scale, and is called the <u>Dominant.</u> The fourth degree is called the <u>Sub-dominant.</u> These three degrees are often referred to by name and are often called the <u>primary</u> or <u>principal</u> triads.

26

The names of all the scale degrees are as follows:

First Degree - Tonic
Second Degree - Supertonic
Third Degree - Mediant
Fourth Degree - Subdominant
Fifth Degree - Dominant
Sixth Degree - Submediant
Seventh Degree - Leading Tone
Eighth Degree - Octave

Chords may be written in different positions. The original position always has the root at the bottom. Other positions are called Inversions.

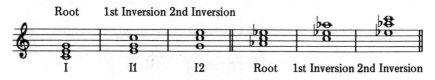

Simple choral harmony is usually written in four voices or parts. One way to do this would be to write the root of each chord in the bass. Since there are only three notes in a Tonic or a Dominant chord, one tone (usually the root) must be doubled. The movement of one chord to another is called a progression. In many progressions there is a common tone. It is usually best to keep the common tone in the same voice.

Examples:

A minor triad is comprised of a minor third and a perfect fifth.

Examples: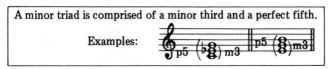

27

Minor Triads occur on the second, II; third, III; and sixth, VI, degrees of the major scale.

The following are various inversions of the minor triads in the key of C Major.

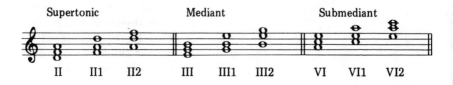

Supertonic   Mediant   Submediant

II   II1   II2   III   III1   III2   VI   VI1   VI2

<u>Remember</u>: a chord is inverted when any note other than the root is in the bass. When the fifth of any triad is in the bass, it is called a six-four chord. Inversions of the minor triads are figured the same as major triads.

An augmented triad is comprised of a major third and an augmented fifth.

Examples: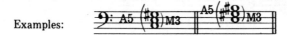

A diminished triad is comprised of a minor third and a diminished fifth.

Examples: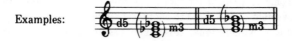

On the following pages a limited amount of information is included about more complex chords. For exercises and drills in the use of these chords or for more detailed information on their use, see Theory and Harmony for Everyone published by Mel Bay Publications, Inc., Pacific, Mo. 63069.

If we add a minor seventh to the Dominant or V chord, it is then called the DOMINANT SEVENTH and is marked V7. The figure 7 may also be used after the letter name. (For example: C7; G7; D7 -)

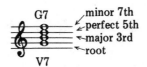

These are
DOMINANT
SEVENTH
CHORDS

minor 7th
perfect 5th
major 3rd
root

FACTS ABOUT THE DOMINANT SEVENTH:
The root of the Dominant Seventh chord may be written in the bass, and is usually doubled in the upper voices. The Dominant triad very often is before the Dominant Seventh. The Dominant Seventh may be repeated in a different position before resolving. Because of the minor seventh interval, the Dominant Seventh chord is more strongly attracted than the Dominant triad, towards the Tonic. It is used more often before the Tonic at the end of a phrase.

The Minor Seventh chord is formed by adding the minor seventh interval to the minor triad. It is composed of a root, a minor third, a perfect fifth, and a minor seventh. The symbol is Am7 or Ami7.

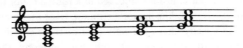

This chord contains both a major triad and its relative minor triad. In the 1st inversion with the 3rd in the bass, it becomes major in quality. In the 2nd and 3rd inversions it is minor in quality as it is, of course, in its original position with the root in the bass.

The Dominant Ninth chord is formed by adding the major ninth interval to the dominant seventh chord. It has the same inversions as the dominant seventh, and may be used instead. In four part harmony, the root, third or fifth is omitted. The ninth is usually found in the top voice, rarely the root.

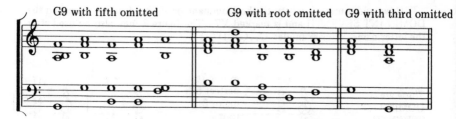

G9 with fifth omitted   G9 with root omitted G9 with third omitted

The <u>Diminished Seventh</u> <u>chord</u> is composed of a root, a minor third, a diminished fifth and a diminished seventh. Example 1 is the correct notation of a Diminished Seventh on C.

Exp. 1

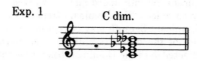

C dim.

Because the correct notation is usually hard to read, "enharmonic equivalents" are used.

Exp. 2

The <u>Augmented Fifth</u> <u>chord</u> is composed of a root, a major third and an augmented fifth. It resolves to the major or minor triad of which the root is the dominant. Enharmonically there are only four of these chords. Therefore any note of the chord could be the root. In four part harmony, the root is usually doubled, sometimes the third, but seldom the fifth. Study the following examples!

Caug. F B♭ aug. E♭ F aug. B♭ G aug. C G aug. C

1st inversion 2nd inversion

Chord Progressions

Traditionally there have been several basic rules governing the progression of chords and chord sequences. To cover this area thoroughly one should use books that are totally devoted to harmony. In this particular book we will mention only the most common of the rules. Composition and harmonization of melodies takes much time and practice. The serious student should continue to work on his own remembering that, except for certain fundamental principles, there are no hard and fast rules.

1. A chord may progress to another chord whose root is either a perfect fourth above or a perfect fifth below. In modern harmony, the VII chord is treated as a V7 chord, with the root missing.
   The progression of chord roots through the cycle of fifths is called Normal or Harmonic. This is often found in a series or sequential pattern.

Exp.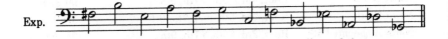

2. A chord may progress to another chord whose root is either a perfect fifth above or a perfect fourth below.

3. All major, minor or seventh chords built on degrees of a major scale are relative to its key.

4. A chord may progress to another chord whose root is either a major or minor third above or a major or minor third below.

5. An accidental in the melody sometimes indicates the third of a new chord. It is usually better to have contrary motion between the bass and melody. This sometimes calls for an inverted chord.

6. A chord may progress to another chord whose root is either a major or minor second above or a major or minor second below. When the root interval is a minor second, the chord progression is usually <u>chromatic</u>.

7. In harmonizing a melody, it should be kept in mind that one should finish with some form of the tonic chord.

Chord Building Chart[*]

Chord Type	Scale Degrees Used	Symbols
Major	Root, 3rd, 5th	Maj
Minor	Root, ♭3rd, 5th	mi, –, m
Diminished	Root, ♭3rd, ♭5th, ♭♭7th	dim, °
Augmented	Root, 3rd, ♯5th	+, aug.
Dominant Seventh	Root, 3rd, 5th, ♭7th	dom. 7, 7
Minor Seventh	Root, ♭3rd, 5th, ♭7th	–7, min 7
Major Seventh	Root, 3rd, 5th, maj. 7th	M7, ma 7
Major Sixth	Root, 3rd, 5th, 6th	M6, M6, 6
Minor Sixth	Root, ♭3rd, 5th, 6th	mi 6, –6
Seventh ♯5th	Root, 3rd, ♯5th, ♭7th	7^{+5}, $7^{♯5}$
Seventh ♭5th	Root, 3rd, ♭5th, ♭7th	7^{-5}, $7^{♭5}$
Major 7th ♭3rd	Root, ♭3rd, 5th, maj. 7th	Ma 7^{-3}
Minor 7th ♭5th	Root, ♭3rd, ♭5th, ♭7th	mi 7^{-5}, $7^{♭5}$
Seventh Suspended 4th	Root, 4th, 5th, ♭7th	7 sus 4
Ninth	Root, 3rd, 5th, ♭7th, 9th	9
Minor Ninth	Root, ♭3rd, 5th, ♭7th, 9th	mi 9, –9
Major Ninth	Root, 3rd, 5th, maj. 7th, 9th	Ma 9
Ninth Augmented 5th	Root, 3rd, ♯5th, ♭7th, 9th	$9^{♯5}$, $9^{♯5}$
Ninth Flatted 5th	Root, 3rd, ♭5th, ♭7th, 9th	9^{-5}, $9^{♭5}$
Seventh ♭9	Root, 3rd, 5th, ♭7th, ♭9th	7^{-9}, $7^{♭9}$
Augmented Ninth	Root, 3rd, 5th, ♭7th, ♯9th	9^{+}, 7^{+9}
9/6	Root, 3rd, 5th, 6th, 9th	$\frac{9}{6}$, 6 add 9
Eleventh	Root, 3rd, 5th, ♭7th, 9th, 11th	11
Augmented Eleventh	Root, 3rd, 5th, ♭7th, 9th, ♯11th	11^{+}, 7 aug 11
Thirteenth	Root, 3rd, 5th, ♭7th, 9th, 11th, 13th	13
Thirteenth ♭9	Root, 3rd, 5th, ♭7th, ♭9th, 11th, 13th	$13^{♭9}$
Thirteenth ♭9♭5	Root, 3rd, ♭5th, ♭7th, ♭9th, 11th, 13th	$13^{♭9\,♭5}$
Half Diminished	Root, ♭3rd, ♭5th, ♭7th	Ø

[*]Note - To arrive at scale degrees above 1 octave (i.e., 9th, 11th, 13th) continue your scale up 2 octaves and keep numbering. The 2nd scale degree will be 9th tone as you begin your second octave.

A Guide to
Music History

The Pre-Renaissance Period
(Before 1450)

Music has been a part of our lives for thousands of years. In fact, there are pictures and writings which tell about music as far back as 4,000 years before the time of Christ. Even in ancient times, people evidently made music of some type almost on a daily basis. It was found in places of worship, in homes; people used music for marching and for work. Thousands of years before the time of Christ, we have evidence that there were choirs of singers who were often accompanied by instrumentalists.

Music was important in the lives of the people in most ancient countries. Music, in fact, was often known as "the language of the gods" and was held sacred. Because of this, we find that sometimes only the priests were allowed to sing and play.

From the Bible, we are able to learn a great deal about the music of the ancient Hebrew people. King David himself was a musician and appointed one tribe of his people to be the "official musicians" of his government. Can you imagine 120 priests blowing trumpets while 4,000 musicians were playing cymbals, harps, psalteries — and at the same time singing? The Bible records such an event. What an impressive experience that must have been!

To some early people, music was magic. It was sung both as a lament for the dead or to celebrate a great victory. As a matter of fact, these people of 3,000 years ago probably used music in about as many ways as we do today.

Specifically, in early Greece, music was always used for feasts and festivals. (The word "music" comes from the Greek "muses.") Thousands of people traveled to music centers each year so that they might hear the great festivals. As a part of the Greek plays, there was a chorus of musicians. There were instrumentalists and, often, soloists. History also shows that the Greeks had professional dancers, as well.

Before we turn completely to the more modern periods of music history, we need to explore briefly the music of the Christian Church from the 4th century on. During the Dark and Middle Ages, the Church was basically in control of all of the arts, including music.

Music, in fact, has always played an important part in the services of the Church. In the early Church, all music was vocal; and the purpose of the melody was to support the meanings of the words. *Gregorian Chant,* or plainsong, was composed as a single-line chant (melody) to be sung in unison without any type of harmony to support it. The rhythm of Gregorian Chant is a free rhythm—similar to speaking to music.

Gregorian Chants, which have been preserved in hundreds of manuscripts, are among the great treasures of Western civilization and stand as a monument to man's religious faith. During the later Middle Ages (from the 9th century on), other voice parts were added to the original chant melodies. This was the beginning of polyphony (many melodies). This type of musical treatment of the Church service reached its highest point in the polyphonic music of Giovanni-Pierluigi da Palestrina, who we will discuss in our look at the Renaissance Period on the next page.

The Renaissance Period
(1450 to 1600)

RENAISSANCE—"Re-birth." The artistic period called the Renaissance was a time during which a glorious flowering of art and music occured. It was also a time of renewed interest in exploring all aspects of living. Musically, vocal music was the most important, and polyphonic music (which we mentioned earlier) was emphasized. New ideas of rhythm and melody were explored. Techniques and mechanics of melody writing were combined, with attention given to the musical ideas and the beauty of the sound.

As was previously stated, the greatest composer of this period was Palestrina. He wrote in almost every style available to him, and his works were often used as models by other composers. No one before Palestrina had brought to music so much beauty and attention to musical detail.

Even though we have talked mostly about the music of the Church (see page 35), the polyphonic music of the Renaissance was not all religious. In the 16th century, secular (non-religious or "popular") polyphonic music came into being. It was livelier and more rhythmic than the music of the Church. The *Madrigal* was one of these early types of "music for fun."

The "point to remember" when discussing the music of the Renaissance is the importance of *polyphony* (many melodies). It is this combination of a number of melodies overlapping by entering and leaving at various times which separates Renaissance music from that which was to come later.

Giovanni-Pierluigi da Palestrina
(1525 to 1594)

Palestrina received his name from the small Italian town near Rome in which he was born in 1525. As a young boy, he sang in the cathedral choir of his native town; but as he became more skilled, he transferred to the choir-school of St. Maria Maggiore in Rome. In 1539 when his voice changed, Palestrina left the choir-school and returned home.

In 1544 he was appointed organist and choir master of the cathedral in his native town. Shortly after, he married and eventually became the father of two sons. About 1551, the Pope made him the choir master of the Julian Chapel at the Vatican. In 1554, Palestrina published a book of Masses, dedicated to the Pope. For this, Palestrina was rewarded by being made a member of the Pope's private chapel choir in 1555. He served only six months in this choir as a change of popes occurred and he was dismissed because of a rule against married singers. In 1571 he became Maestro of the Cappella Giulia, retaining this position until his death.

In 1584, Palestrina brought out his settings of *The Song of Solomon,* and his harmonized version of *The Latin Hymnal* was published. His Mass entitled *Pope Marcellus Mass* was considered to be his best work and was used as a standard by which all other works of this type were judged. He died in 1594 and was buried in the Cappella Nuova of old St. Peter's.

Although Palestrina's music was always sung in the Sistine Chapel in the Vatican, it otherwise fell into general neglect for almost 200 years after his death. In the 1800s, a revival of interest began; and modern editions of his music were published.

Composers before Palestrina seemed to hold very strictly to the prevailing rules of composition. Although Palestrina knew the rules, the *beauty* of the composition was his first thought. Of course, Palestrina's many works were all polyphonic, the style of writing that was so very important in the music of the Renaissance Period.

The Baroque Period
(1600 to 1750)

The Baroque Era was a time of magnificence and splendor in architecture, music, and art. It was also a time of intense religious feeling and a time of devastation and destruction in Europe. (Germany was involved in the 30 Years War.)

Art and music were supported largely by wealthy nobility and by the Church. Noblemen and clergymen were both well educated, and they were interested in the arts and sciences. The ruling families throughout Europe were responsible for much of the cultural development during this time.

In fact, artists and musicians could not have existed without being paid by a wealthy nobleman or official of the Church. Artworks were frequently created for a specific purpose, either to decorate a building or for a special occasion. The arts, therefore, fulfilled a practical purpose and gave artistic pleasure as well.

George Frederic Handel, one of the leading composers of the Baroque Period, was often commissioned by King George I of England to compose music for special social events. It was common for London newspapers to mention Handel on both the society pages and the pages devoted to news.

German church music of the Baroque Period was greatly influenced by chorales (or hymns) of the German Protestant Church. Many of these tunes were melodies the people already knew placed with words that were more suitable for the church service. These hymns were usually harmonized so that they could be sung in parts by both choirs and congregations. Johann Sebastian Bach was one of many Baroque composers who wrote hymns and chorale tunes for the Church.

George Frederic Handel and Johann Sebastian Bach were two of the most important composers of the Baroque Era. During this period, as in the Renaissance, musicians were thought of as servants; nevertheless, they enjoyed a certain independence since musicians were also frequently organized into musician guilds.

The guilds regulated training and worked to uphold the rights of their members. Through the guilds, standards of excellence were maintained in the musical profession. Both Bach and Handel were members of the guilds and followed their training schedule to become master musicians. These two composers created many of the outstanding musical masterpieces from this period of history.

SOME GENERAL CHARACTERISTICS OF BAROQUE MUSIC ARE:

MELODY: A single melodic idea.
RHYTHM: Continuous rhythmic drive.
TEXTURE: Balance of homophonic (melody with chordal harmony) and polyphonic textures.
TIMBRE: Orchestral — strings, winds (and harpsichord) with very little percussion.
DYNAMICS: Abrupt shifts from loud to soft—achieved by adding or subtracting instruments.

An overall characteristic of Baroque music is that a single musical piece tended to project a single mood or expression of feeling.

Johann Sebastian Bach
(1685 to 1750)

Bach was the first great musician to disregard the rules of harmony and rhythm that were strictly followed by other composers. This fact alone helped to make him the forerunner of musical composition as we know it today. Born the son of a violinist in Eisenach, Germany in 1685, he received his first musical training on the violin.

At the age of 10, he went to live in the home of his brother, Christoph, who taught Johann to play the harpsichord and the organ. It was also at this time that Bach began school, where his boy-soprano voice was greatly admired and appreciated. When his voice changed, Bach concentrated on the violin; but the organ soon took his interest and he decided to devote himself to church music.

At the age of 18, Bach became the organist at Arnstadt and began his work in musical composition. After a short period of time, he moved to Muhlhausen where he married his cousin, Maria Bach. At Muhlhausen he began to experiment with changes in the music used in the church services of the German Protestant Church. It was also during this time that he began to become somewhat well known. It was this that gained for him the position as court organist and violinist to the duke at

Weimar, where he remained for about nine years. During this nine-year period, he wrote many cantatas for the Church, suites for the clavichord and harpsichord, and fugues (musical compositions in which the first melody is continually repeated and imitated throughout the entire piece). In fact, because he wrote so many fugues for the organ and piano, he is often called "the Great Master of the Fugue."

His next position at Kothen was the period in which he produced much of his orchestral music and music for the clavichord and harpsichord. In 1720 his wife died; and a year later he married Anna Wulken, who was also a musician. She evidently helped him considerably in his work.

In 1723 Bach went to Leipzig as music director of the Thomas-schule. During his stay at Leipzig, he wrote many of his church cantatas and oratorios. Among these is his famous *Christmas Oratorio*. In 1749 Bach became totally blind; and in the following year, 1750, he died.

Historians tell us that Bach did not seem to associate very much with other musicians and was far more interested in his family of 20 children and in composing and directing his church choirs than in becoming "famous." In addition to his almost unequaled skill as a composer, he also was an excellent organ builder, as well as an expert music copyist.

Since most of his life was spent within a few miles of his birthplace, we also now know that Bach's music was not widely known throughout the world during his lifetime. In fact, many of Bach's most beautiful works were unpublished and unperformed for almost 100 years, until two later composers (Mendelssohn and Schumann) discovered the beauties of his music and began to perform them and make them known to the world.

George Frederic Handel

(1685 to 1759)

George Frederic Handel was born at Halle, Germany, in 1685. His father, who was not a musician, wanted Handel to become a lawyer and opposed his desire to study music. Nevertheless, Handel, without his father's knowledge or approval, taught himself to play the harpsichord.

Finally, at the age of 7, his father allowed him to study music. Lessons were arranged; and, by the age of 11, Handel played the harpsichord, organ, violin, and oboe. By this time, he had also composed six sonatas for two oboes and bass and was the assistant organist to his teacher at Halle Cathedral.

In 1702 he entered Halle University and started studying law. However, he continued to hold a position as a church organist. One year later, Handel joined an orchestra in Hamburg; and, at the age of 20, he wrote his first opera, *Almira.*

In 1707 Handel visited Italy and then wrote his first Italian opera. Shortly thereafter, the production of his opera *Agrippina* in Venice spread his fame throughout Italy.

Handel returned to Germany around 1710 to become choir master to the elector of Hanover, but shortly traveled to London, where a production of one of his operas was so successful that he was asked to remain in England. Handel decided to return to Germany; but, on his next visit to London in 1712, he wrote, among other things, *An Ode for the Queen's Birthday,* which won him such public and royal favor that he was given an annual salary of several hundred pounds.

Within a very short period, his former employer, the elector of Hanover, became King George I of England. Handel's famous *Water Music* was written for George I for a festival on the River Thames. The King so greatly enjoyed the music that, from that time until he died, Handel received a salary from the British court.

In 1720 Handel was appointed director of the Royal Academy of Music in London, where he produced a large number of operas. Many of these works were considered "failures," so he finally redirected his attention to oratorios and composed the works for which he is now best known. Handel's oratorios were written after he was 53 years old. The most famous of these, "Messiah," was written in less than a month's time.

At one of the first London performances of *Messiah,* King George I was so inspired by the "Hallelujah Chorus" that he stood up. The entire audience followed his example, which began the present custom of standing when the "Hallelujah Chorus" is sung.

Handel became almost totally blind six years before his death, but continued to perform until he died. He was a naturalized British subject and, when he died in 1759, was buried in Westminster Abbey in London.

The Classical Period
(1750 to 1825)

The term "Classical music" specifically refers to music written during a period of music history dating from about 1750 to 1825. Because much of the activity of the great classical composers — Haydn, Mozart, and Beethoven — centered around Vienna, Austria, it is often called the "Viennese-Classical Period." The Classical Period was an attempt to reject the highly complex and ornamented music and art of the Baroque Period. Classicism can best be described as having qualities of balance and order.

During the Classical Period, three great revolutions took place in the world: the Industrial Revolution, the American Revolution, and the French Revolution. The Industrial Revolution, triggered by the invention of the steam engine, stimulated manufacturing and commerce and enabled the middle class to gain wealth and influence. Both the American and French Revolutions were challenges to the ruling monarchies and served to improve the lot of the common man. By the end of the 18th century, the power of kings all over the world had been greatly reduced.

This change had its effect on musicians. At the beginning of the Classical Period, musicians were still dependent on the wealthy and the Church; and they were considered to be in the servant class. Gradually, this began to change, and by 1800 composers were writing mainly for the general public.

The music of the Classical Period, as in all periods of history, reflects the society from which it comes. Life during the Classical Period was elegant and formal. The people dressed in elaborate clothes and wigs. The furniture and homes were designed for their formal beauty. It stands to reason, then, that the music of Haydn and Mozart, as well as the earlier compositions of Beethoven, tended to follow rather formal structures.

One of the most important forms of music to come into being during the Classical Period was the string quartet — that is, music written for first and second violin, viola, and cello. An important feature of these compositions was that none of them contained a part for the harpsichord. This was important because, in the Baroque Period, the harpsichord was almost always used to strengthen the harmony. The Classical string quartet was the string quartet as we know it today. Most of the major composers since that time have written for that particular medium.

SOME GENERAL CHARACTERISTICS OF CLASSICAL MUSIC ARE:

MELODY: Short and clearly defined musical phrases with two or more contrasting themes.

RHYTHM: Very defined and regular.

TEXTURE: Mostly homophonic.

TIMBRE: The symphony orchestra was organized into four sections—strings, woodwinds, brass, and percussion. The harpsichord was very seldom used.

Franz Joseph Haydn

(1732 to 1809)

Franz Joseph Haydn was born in Rohrau, Austria, in 1732. By the age of 5, Haydn obviously had musical talent; and he was sent to study with a relative living close to Vienna. When Haydn was 8 years old, he became a member of the famous choir at St. Stephen's Cathedral in Vienna. For nine years he sang both at the cathedral and in the homes of the nobility.

When Haydn was dismissed from the choir at the age of 17, he turned to other forms of music. His main interest was the harpsichord and violin, but he also studied composition thoroughly. By the age of 27, he was well known throughout Vienna. It was during this period of his musical life that he wrote his first Mass and first string quartet.

Because he was so well known, Haydn caught the attention of the famous Hungarian noble family of Esterházy. Haydn was only 29 when he entered their service as the assistant conductor of the orchestra. Two years later he was made conductor. Under his direction, it soon became one of the finest private orchestras of that time.

In 1790 Prince Nikolaus Esterházy died, and Haydn was dismissed from service. He immediately visited London for the purpose of giving a series of concerts. He was received with such enthusiasm that Oxford University conferred on him an Honorary Doctorate of Music. Some of his best orchestral works were written during this time in England. "The Clock," "The Surprise," and "The London" are today considered some of the best of his symphonies.

In 1795 Haydn returned to Austria and was honored throughout the country. It was not long after this that he wrote "The Emperor's Hymn," which became the Austrian national anthem. He continued writing until his death in 1809.

It was Haydn's achievement in the instrumental music field that earned for him his place in music history. In fact, he has often been called "the Father of the Symphony" because his symphonic works so overshadowed the works of those who came before him.

Wolfgang Amadeus Mozart
(1756 to 1791)

Wolfgang Amadeus Mozart, born at Salzburg, Austria, in 1756, began taking lessons from his musician father at age 4; and at age 5 he began to compose. Mozart learned so quickly that in 1762 his father took him to Munich and Vienna to introduce him to the public. It was at this same time that Mozart learned to play the violin without any instruction. It is also said that he did the same thing on the organ after someone explained the use of the pedals to him.

The following year, when Mozart was 7, the entire family traveled to Paris, where he had his first compositions published. In 1764, while visiting in England, he composed several sonatas for violin and harpsichord and a number of symphonies. Mozart was only 8 years old. In 1769, on a visit to Rome, history tells us that Mozart went to hear the Sistine choir sing; and, after returning home, he put the entire work on paper from memory. Before he was 25 years old, he had visited most of the great cities of Europe.

Mozart's father was in service to the Archbishop of Salzburg most of his life, so Mozart was appointed concert-master to the archbishop for a short time. Mozart was never able to accept the role of servant very well, however; so, after a number of differences of opinion, he was dismissed in 1781. From then on, he was basically "on his own."

In 1782 he married Constance Weber, the cousin of another great composer, Carl Maria Von Weber. It was during their life together, much of which was spent in poverty, that his three great operas, *Don Giovanni, The Magic Flute,* and *The Marriage of Figaro,* were written. The writing of his last work, "The Requiem," was not finished at his death. Mozart died in Vienna and was buried in a "pauper's grave," the exact spot not known.

Mozart's productivity was astounding, and he wrote in virtually every style available to him. His experience all over Europe and his contact with the different musical styles made his works typical of the entire European musical situation as it was during his lifetime.

Ludwig van Beethoven
(1770 to 1827)

Beethoven was born in 1770 in Bonn, the city on the Rhine River which is now the capital of West Germany. Both his grandfather and his father were professional musicians. Beethoven began music lessons in violin, piano, and composition with his father when he was 4 years old. This arrangement continued until he was 9. In addition to this, he attended the public school in Bonn until he was 14.

When he was quite young, Beethoven could improvise ("make up" music on the spur of the moment) very well on the piano; and in 1781 he composed his first published composition. A year later he began his first "paying job" as assistant court organist in Bonn. Beethoven also played second viola in both the theatre and church orchestras.

At the age of 17, Beethoven met Mozart on a visit to Vienna. Mozart was so impressed with his ability to improvise and his performance skills that he supposedly said, "He will give the world something worth listening to."

In 1792 Haydn met Beethoven in Bonn and was extremely complimentary of his work. This so impressed the elector (the governor) that Beethoven was sent to Vienna to study. It was in Vienna that he took lessons from Haydn.

Around 1800, Beethoven began to notice that he was becoming deaf; and by 1820 his deafness had increased to the point that he could no longer conduct his orchestra. Although completely deaf for the last seven years of his life, he continued to write. Some of his greatest compositions were produced during this time. He died in Vienna in 1827.

Beethoven wrote in practically all musical forms, but is one of the greatest of all instrumental composers. His works include one opera, an oratorio, two Masses, various songs, as well as sonatas for piano and for the violin. His concertos include five for the piano and one for the violin.

His nine symphonies are considered his greatest works. His ninth symphony was revolutionary in that he used a large choir with the orchestra in the last movement. On its first performance, the audience responded with wild applause; but Beethoven could not hear them. Only when the concert master turned him around did he see how enthusiastically it was received. It has been said that his third symphony was Beethoven's favorite, but his fifth symphony is the most popular today.

The Romantic Period
(1825 to 1900)

The Romantic Period in music occurred during a time of great social, political, and economic change. As a result of the American Revolution, the French Revolution, and the Industrial Revolution, the whole structure of society was changed. From a society of farms and small cities where the wealth was held by the nobility and the Church, an industrial society of factories and cities grew. This new society was controlled by "the new middle class." No longer did a man have to be a servant unless he chose to be one. Now he could raise himself up as high as his own abilities or initiative would take him.

The Romantic ideas spread throughout Europe and influenced both art and music. Instead of emphasizing logic and controlled emotions, the "Romantics" placed a great importance on personal feelings and emotions. They were interested in the unusual and the fantastic. Romantic composers were concerned with self-expression, and they felt that the Classical forms were too binding for them. Consequently, they either created new forms or changed those that were used before.

Romanticism found expression in many musical forms which included the symphony, the concerto, the opera, the art song, the solo piano piece, and the symphonic poem. One of the most characteristic Romantic forms was the *art song,* and the great Romantic composer who was known for his art songs was Franz Schubert. Few composers have had Schubert's gift for melody. He believed a song should express emotions both through the words and the music.

The piano was the favorite instrument of many Romantic composers because it was an instrument on which some of the distinctive qualities of Romantic music could be expressed. One of the greatest composers of piano music during the 1800s was Frederick Chopin, who wrote almost entirely for this instrument. Chopin explored the piano's possibilities through his preludes, waltzes, etudes (studies), and impromptus with remarkable originality. He developed a harmonic and a melodic style that strongly influenced composers for years after his death.

In short, the Romantic Period in music was exciting and revolutionary. Probably more than half of the serious music heard in concert halls today comes from composers of this period of music history. New styles of compositions became the norm and indeed continue to dominate today's concert halls. In the opinion of many, the Romantic Period was the "Golden Age" of concert music.

SOME GENERAL CHARACTERISTICS OF ROMANTIC MUSIC ARE:

MELODY: Long, lyrical melodies with irregular phrases; wide, somewhat angular skips; extensive use of chromaticism; vivid contrasts; a variety of melodic ideas within one movement.

RHYTHM: Frequent changes in both tempo and meter.

TEXTURE: Almost entirely homophonic.

TIMBRE: A great variety of tone color; woodwind and brass sections of the orchestra increased; many special orchestral effects introduced; rich and colorful orchestration.

Franz Schubert
(1797 to 1828)

Franz Schubert was born in 1797 near Vienna. His family was rather poor, since his father was a schoolmaster. Schubert received his first musical instruction from his father, an amateur cellist, and was taught violin beginning at the age of 8. By the time he was 11, he began lessons on the piano, organ, and in voice. In fact, Schubert's voice was so beautiful that he was quickly admitted into the Imperial Choir and the training school for the court singers. In this school, he was taught theory and was the first violinist in the orchestra. Occasionally, Schubert was allowed to conduct.

After studying instrumental composition, he wrote his first symphony in 1813. The following year he completed his first Mass (1814). In order to escape being forced into the military, he took a job as elementary teacher in his father's school. It was during these years that he began to compose with great rapidity. His entire "leisure" time was devoted to composition. In 1815 he wrote his famous art song, "Erl King." In 1816 he left the school and went to Vienna, where he spent the remainder of his life.

Schubert's fondness for parties, his unbusinesslike habits, and his lack of attention to day-to-day living made his life a struggle for existence. Like Beethoven, Schubert never married; and, beautiful as his music is, it was not appreciated during his lifetime. He died in Vienna at the age of 31 and was buried near Beethoven, whom he greatly admired.

Schubert had the least formal training of all the great German musicians of his time, but his keen musical mind and his fantastic melodic gift made up for the lack of formal education. He is famous as the creator of German art songs, of which he wrote over 600. Two of his best-known art songs are "Serenade" and "Ave Maria." Many people feel that he contributed more to the development of the art song than any other composer in history.

Schubert wrote several dramatic works but was not overly successful in this style. He also wrote chamber music and piano music, as well as for choir. He composed eight symphonies, the most famous one being the "Unfinished Symphony." This symphony was never performed during Schubert's lifetime and is "unfinished" only in the sense that it has only two movements instead of the normal four.

His "Symphony in C Major," which some consider his greatest, was never heard by the composer, either. It was not until 11 years after his death that it was performed under Felix Mendelssohn.

Felix Mendelssohn
(1809 to 1847)

Born in Hamburg, Germany in 1809, the son of a wealthy banker, Felix Mendelssohn had none of the financial worries common to many other famous composers. Like Mozart and Beethoven, his musical talent was noticeable at an early age. Everything possible was done to give him the best of training. Felix first received instruction on the piano from his mother and also studied theory and violin. By the time he was 10, Mendelssohn played in public. At 12 he could compose remarkably well.

When Felix was only 17, he wrote an overture to Shakespeare's *A Midsummer Night's Dream,* which is thought by some to be the most beautiful musical work written by anyone that young. His first and only real opera was performed in Berlin in 1827. In 1829, with the performance of the *St. Matthew Passion,* he drew attention to Bach's compositions, as this was the first performance of Bach's works anywhere since his death in 1750.

At about this time, Mendelssohn made his first trip to England and not only conducted his "Symphony in C Minor" as well as a number of other major works, but also established himself as an excellent pianist and a fine organist. Following this concert season, Mendelssohn began a series of tours which took him to Scotland, Austria, Germany, Italy, Switzerland, and then to Paris, France.

It is generally acknowledged that Mendelssohn was one of the first to write independent concert overtures. Before this, overtures were written as musical introductions to operas or oratorios, while the concert-overture, as developed by Mendelssohn, is complete in itself.

From 1833 to 1835, Mendelssohn conducted important festivals throughout Germany. In 1835 he became conductor of the famous Gewandhaus Orchestra. He married in 1837 (and became the father of five children), and in 1843 he founded the Leipzig Conservatory — one of the most famous of all music schools. In 1846, while in England, Mendelssohn conducted his most famous oratorio, *Elijah*. He was greatly admired by the English and is considered to have made a greater impression on English music than any other composer, with perhaps the exception of Handel.

On returning from a trip to England in 1847, Mendelssohn learned of his sister's death — a shock from which he never recovered. He died shortly in Leipzig and was buried in Berlin.

His music, filled with original beauty and clearness of melodic expression, consists of symphonies, overtures, concertos, music for different combinations of string instruments, piano compositions, organ music, and his famous oratorios, *St. Paul* and *Elijah*.

Frederic Chopin
(1810 to 1849)

Frederic Chopin was born in 1810 in a small village near Warsaw, Poland. It was here that Chopin began his general education. Although he did study music with professional teachers, he was in a sense self-taught. When he was only 9 years old, his talent was so pronounced that Chopin played a piano concerto in public. His first published work (in 1825) was a rondo (a composition consisting of one principle theme which appears again and again, alternating with other themes).

In 1829, already a composer who was somewhat known and a polished player, Chopin set out for London by way of Vienna, Munich, and Paris. His first concert in Paris was given to a select audience of musicians who were so impressed that he did not go on to London. He remained in Paris for the remainder of his life. Not only did Chopin make a deep and lasting impression in Paris, but he was a very close friend of men like Franz Liszt, as well as other famous musicians and artists.

From the beginning of his life in Paris, he taught piano. Chopin had an intense dislike for public concerts, so his yearly concerts were for the musical elite only. Occasionally, he would play in certain private homes. Robert Schumann, reviewing some of his works in 1839, wrote a glowing article in which he praised Chopin highly.

Chopin, through Liszt, first met the novelist George Sand in 1836 and fell deeply in love. He believed she was the source of his inspiration. In 1838 he developed a severe case of bronchitis from which he never recovered. When his sickness turned into tuberculosis, he and George Sand parted. Disregarding his failing health, Chopin visited Great Britain in 1848 and again in 1849. Very sick and depressed, he returned to Paris in 1849 to die.

To Chopin goes much credit for treating the piano as a solo instrument. Chopin was dreamy and poetical. His music, mostly written for the piano, expressed his thoughts and feelings. Its sadness was probably the outcome of his brooding over the destruction of Poland. Occasionally, perhaps because of his life in Paris, his music portrayed happiness and tenderness. His playing was perfect; his technique brilliant; and the interpretation of his own works outstanding. Chopin was the perfect Romanticist.

Franz Liszt
(1811 to 1886)

Franz Liszt, famous pianist and composer, was born in Hungary in 1811, the son of a steward on one of Prince Esterhá zy's estates. Liszt began studying piano at the age of 6 with his father. Franz's progress was so rapid that, at the age of 9, he played his first public concert. The family moved to Vienna in 1821, where Franz studied piano and theory. When he was only

11, he gave a concert which won great praise from Beethoven himself.

These Viennese concerts were so successful that the elder Liszt decided to take Franz to Paris to study at the Conservatory. Admission was refused, though, because of a rule forbidding the entrance of foreigners. However, Liszt continued to study composition.

His father's death in 1827 forced Liszt to support his mother and himself. He decided to settle in Paris, where he was in great demand as a teacher. When he was 28, Franz set out on a concert tour of Europe, which brought him not only recognition as the greatest pianist of his day, but also considerable wealth. In 1849 Liszt accepted the position of music director of the court at Weimar, which he held for ten years.

The next period of his life was spent in Rome, where he studied for the Church. In 1866 the Pope conferred on him the title of Father. The remainder of his life was spent in Rome, with several months of each summer spent at Weimar. While attending a Wagner festival at Bayreuth in 1886, Liszt was taken quite ill and died a few weeks later.

Liszt's life may be divided into two periods. The first was that in which he devoted himself almost exclusively to the piano. Most of his original piano works and his transcriptions and arrangements on works of other composers belong to this period. The second period started with the ten years of Weimar. Here he devoted himself to composition in the larger forms. His own symphonic poems were written during this time. In fact, most people give him credit for begin the creator of the symphonic poem (a musical setting of a story, free in style — and usually in only one movement). The Hungarian rhapsodies, his cantatas, piano concertos, Masses, and short works for orchestra and piano were composed during these later years.

Johannes Brahms
(1833 to 1897)

Brahms, born in Hamburg, Germany, came from a family which for generations had been interested in music. Brahms's father, a musician himself, gave Brahms his first musical instruction. Brahms was a willing and earnest student who at the age of 14 made his piano debut — playing his own variations on a folk song.

When he was 20, Brahms made a concert tour with violinist Remenyi. It was on this tour that he met Robert Schumann. Brahms's talent so impressed Schumann that he wrote an article in an important music journal naming Brahms as "the coming hero among composers." Schumann and his wife, Clara, remained his lifelong friends.

For four years he held a position as music director at the court of a German prince. After that, Brahms lived in various places and made concert tours which brought him artistic and financial success. He finally settled in Vienna in 1878. From that time on, Vienna was his home; and he died there in 1897.

Brahms never married. In his youth he was a brilliant pianist, and his first published music was for piano. He wrote every type of music except opera. He was patient and worked endlessly on his compositions, as was exemplified by the fact that he worked ten years, off and on, on his first symphony. Brahms was 43 when his first symphony was published in 1877, and it created a great sensation.

Brahms wrote with amazing technical skill, but his handling of the instruments was criticized by some as being not of the highest degree. Some critics also thought that he stressed the perfection of musical form far too much. This fact led some to say that his music tended to be heavy and dead at times.

Among Brahms's works are his four symphonies, smaller orchestral pieces, concertos, chamber music, piano music, many art songs, choral works, and choral-orchestral compositions. His *German Requiem* was the work said by many to have established his fame.

Peter Ilitch Tchaikovsky
(1840 to 1893)

Tschaikovsky was born in Russia in 1840. He received piano lessons from his fourth to his tenth year, but none of his teachers saw any future in music for him. He then studied law and was graduated from law school at the age of 19.

He disliked law, though, and thought it boring; so at the age of 22 he entered the conservatory at St. Petersburg, where he studied under Rubinstein. Rubinstein, in 1866, hired Tschaikovsky as a professor of harmony at his new conservatory which he opened in Moscow. Tschaikovsky's position at the conservatory gave him time to write his first few symphonies, as well as other shorter compositions.

Shortly after moving to Moscow, his strange friendship began with Nadejda von Meck — an elderly and wealthy widow. Mrs. von Meck commissioned him for works for which she paid huge fees. The two never met, but carried on their friendship through letters. Tschaikovsky spent considerable time at the different von Meck estates when Mrs. von Meck was not there.

Tschaikovsky was a very shy man, but in 1877 he decided to marry. His marriage ended shortly thereafter and was a complete and tragic failure. This failure sent him into a state of near nervous collapse, so he moved to Switzerland to recover. Mrs. von Meck then offered him an annual income, which left him free to compose and travel as he desired. His fourth symphony was composed soon after this incident and reflects his apparently happy mental state. in 1878 he became director of the Moscow branch of the Russian Music Society.

Tschaikovsky's first public appearance as a conductor came in 1887 when he gave a concert of his own works at St. Petersburg. The following year, the Russian czar also began a yearly allowance. In addition, this was the year in which he made his first tour — conducting concerts in Germany, Prague, Paris, and London. Tchaikovsky also visited America in 1891 and conducted a concert at the dedication of Carnegie Hall. Six other very successful concerts were given in several other American cities, as well. He died in 1893.

Although Tschaikovsky was Russian, his music was not limited to that which sounds Russian. His music tends to be more universal and has strange and fierce contrasts of mood. In addition, his orchestrations show an excellent understanding of the orchestra. Tschaikovsky composed many songs, some operas, ballet music, various types of orchestral works, and chamber music; but most agree that his fame stems from his symphonies.

The Impressionist Period
(1885 to 1910)

In the late 19th century, we find a few composers rebelling against the rules of Romantic music. This was due in part to the result of a political conflict. In 1870 France was defeated by Germany in the Franco-Prussian War. The French people reacted by turning away from everything German and by emphasizing everything French. The result was an entirely new kind of musical and artistic expression. This movement came to be known as *Impressionism.*

The German composers loved to express themselves in musical works on a grand scale — operas with large casts and symphonies that lasted more than an hour. The French, mainly through the musical works of Claude Debussy, revolted against "bigness" and tried to break many of the so-called "rules" of musical composition.

The Impressionist painters were concerned with changing light and color rather than with heroic subjects. The emphasis was on catching a quick impression rather than creating an exact likeness. Influenced by the French painters, Debussy attempted to translate some of their effects into music.

One of the techniques he used to capture a vague, dreamlike quality was to break down the feeling of attraction to a tonal center. Debussy used a scale in which all tones are the same distance apart. Consequently, in his "whole-tone scale," as he called it, no tone acts as a tonal center. (In other words, there is no "key.") Some people have likened Impressionistic music to objects seen dimly through a fog or through a sheer curtain. In short, Impressionistic music establishes a mood or a feeling, rather than telling a story.

Claude Debussy
(1862 to 1917)

The search for a new musical style at the end of the 19th century was evident everywhere, but it seemed to show itself most clearly in France through the music of Claude Debussy. Debussy wrote in the highly individual style we now call "the Impressionistic style." This means the expression through music of what one actually experiences or imagines.

Claude Debussy was born in France in 1862; and while he was still very young he was sent to the Paris Conservatory, where he won many prizes for sight singing, piano, and composition. At the age of 22, he was awarded the Grand Prix de Rome. Debussy constantly worked on new ideas and a new style. However, the compositions he wrote were severely criticized. Most of the critics and professors of that day observed strict musical form and rules and did not approve of Debussy's work. The fact that he had developed beautiful pieces of music was not important to these critics.

In 1894 Debussy wrote a tone poem, "The Afternoon of a Faun," which created much talk and a lot of criticism. In fact, during the following years, Debussy wrote many things of great significance. Some which are outstanding are: two volumes of *Preludes for Piano, Images, La Mer, Nocturnes,* and others.

The last years of Debussy's life were spent under physical and financial hardship. A victim of cancer, he kept on working; but his financial problems brought on by World War I caused him great stress. In 1918 he died. It was quite some time later, however, before the world realized that Debussy, one of France's greatest musicians, was no longer living.

The Contemporary Period
(1900 to Present)

Almost unbelievable developments in the sciences, occurring at an increasing rate, are changing mankind. Exploration, discovery, and technological advances in mathematics, chemistry, physics, bacteriology, and in the other sciences are responsible for changing the nature of life in the 20th century. All of the arts, reflecting the society in which they exist, have also undergone radical changes and have taken many new directions.

For example, since 1900, there have been composers who gradually broke away from the rules of musical composition and used discordant harmony and irregular melodies in their writing. The form or style of composition changed, as well. Composers began using special musical effects of all types. Some worked for realism, while others worked with "abstract music" — music without a story — music which required a "thinking musician" to perform (or even to appreciate).

The break with tradition in the last 80 or 90 years has been radical and very conspicuous. To understand the changes that music has undergone in the 20th century is almost impossible; but, by studying the following general characteristics and by listening to the music of such contemporary composers as George Gershwin, Charles Ives, Aaron Copland, Dimitri Shostakovich, among others, one can begin to determine the degree to which modern music is different from or similar to the music of previous periods.

SOME GENERAL CHARACTERISTICS OF CONTEMPORARY MUSIC ARE:

(Contemporary compositions vary widely, so this is not a complete list; and not all of these characteristics are present in every composition.)

1. Fewer lyrical melodies than the music of former periods.
2. Dissonant harmonies.
3. Complex rhythms.
4. Percussiveness.
5. Greater use of woodwind, brass, and percussion instruments than in music of earlier periods.
6. The use of synthetic and electronic sounds.

Into the Next Century

We have now traced the history of music through the composers of the Renaissance, Baroque, Classical, Romantic, and Contemporary Periods. We have discovered that music is everyone's language. In addition, we have found that often, when we play a tune or sing a song, we are unable to tell the nationality, the color, the religion, or the politics of the person who wrote it. Music is universal.

Looking back into past periods of composition, we find that people usually accept music several years after it is first written. For example, the music of Bach was not well known for almost 100 years after he wrote it. The lives of the men included in this book are still influencing our lives because of the music which they wrote.

It is difficult to tell what the new classification will be for "modern" composers. Some are called Ultramodern or Avant Garde because they follow few, if any, rules. To some, their compositions sound like noise. As we see and hear computer music, the increasing use of synthesizers, pure electronic music, as well as much of our popular music, it becomes very clear that changes are coming extremely fast. Some of the new material will endure; much of it will not. Only time will tell.

M.Honegger

A Musical
Dictionary

— A —

A — The sixth note of the diatonic major scale of C.
A cappella (It.) — Unaccompanied vocal music.
Accelerando (It.) — Gradually increasing the rate of speed.
Accent — A strong emphasis upon a certain tone, chord, or beat.
Accessory notes — Notes which are situated one degree above and one degree below the principle note of a tune. The upper note of a trill is also called the accessory note.
Accidentals — Sharps, flats, or naturals which are not found in the key signature.
Adagietto (It.) — Not as slowly as adagio.
Adagio (It.) — Slowly. Also a movement written in this time (slowly).
Adagio cantabile (It.) — Very slow and sustained.
Agitato (It.) — A very restless and agitated style of playing or singing.
Al fine (It.) — To the end.
Alla breve — Originally 4/2 meter. Now, 4/4 time at a faster rate of speed and usually counted as 2/2.
Allegretto (It.) — Slightly slower than allegro.
Allegro (It.) — Very quickly, although not as fast as presto.
Allegro con moto (It.) — Fast; with movement.
Allegro moderato (It.) — Moderately fast.
Allegro vivace (It.) — Quite fast and in a vivacious manner.
Al segno (It.) — Return to the sign.
Alto (It.) — Originally this term was applied to high male voices. Presently it is generally used to refer to the lowest female voice.
Alto clef — The C clef on the third line of the staff. This clef is used for the viola, alto trombone, and often for the alto voice.
Andante (It.) — A movement in moderate time.
Andante cantabile (It.) — Slowly and sustained.
Andante sostenuto (It.) — In a slow and sustained manner.
Andantino (It.) — Literally, slightly slower than andante.
Animato (It.) — Animated and lively.
A poco (It.) — Gradually or by degrees.
Appoggiatura (It.) — A grace note or a note of embellishment.
Aria (It.) — An air or a song sung by a single voice either with or without accompaniment.
Arioso (It.) — In a singing style or in the style of an aria.
Arpeggio (It.) — A term applied to the notes of a chord played consecutively.
Arrangement — A selection or adaptation of a composition to instruments or voices for which it was not originally written.
Articulation — Distinct pronunciation.
A tempo (It.) — In time.
Attack — A firm and clear entry of voices or instruments at the beginning of a phrase.
Augmented — 1) An interval greater than perfect or major; 2) a theme or melody written in notes of greater value than in its original form.
Authentic cadence — The traditional name for a perfect cadence in which the harmony of the dominant is followed by that of the tonic.
Auxiliary scales — Scales in relative keys.

— B —

B — The seventh note in the scale of C.
Bagpipe — An ancient wind instrument now usually thought of as being from Scotland.
Ballad — A short, simple song designed to suit a popular audience.
Ballet (Fr.) — A theatrical representation of a story told in dancing and pantomime.
Banjo — A five-string instrument with sound reinforced by a parchment-covered hoop.
Bar — A line drawn from the top to the bottom of a staff which shows the division of the time in a piece of music. A bar divides the music into measures.
Bar, double — Heavy double barlines drawn vertically through the staff, usually designating the end of a section or a composition.

Baritone — A male voice between the bass and tenor.

Barre (Fr.) — In lute or guitar playing, the stopping of several or all of the strings with the left-hand forefinger.

Bass clef — The F clef on the fourth line of the staff.

Bass tuba — A brass instrument of very low pitch with a range of four octaves.

Bass voice — The lowest male voice.

Basso continuo — A system of harmony developed in the 1600's using a figured bass.

Basso ostinato (It.) — Ground bass; a bass figure which is constantly repeated.

Bassoon — A woodwind instrument of the oboe family with a range of three octaves.

Baton (Fr.) — A conductor's stick or wand.

Beat — The rise or fall of the hand or baton in marking the divisions of time in music.

Bel canto (It.) — Refers to singing in a pure, tender, legato style.

Bell — 1) The flaring end of the tube of various wind instruments; 2) a hollow instrument, set in vibration by a clapper inside or a hammer outside.

Binary — Twofold; a form of two divisions, periods, or sections; two beats to a measure.

Bow — Made of wood and horsehair and used to set strings in vibration.

Bowing — The art of using the bow; playing the bow.

Brace — A mark connecting two or more staves together.

Breve (It.) — 1) short; 2) the breve is now the longest note or double whole note.

Bridge — A piece of wood on instruments with a soundboard which performs a double duty of raising the strings and of terminating at one end their vibrating portion.

Broken chords — Arpeggios.

— C —

C — The first note of the natural scale.

C clef — The clef which shows the position of middle C. This clef is used for the soprano, alto, and tenor parts.

Cadence (Fr.) — The end of a phrase, either in the melody or the harmony.

Cadenza (It.) — An ornamental passage usually introduced towards the end of the first and/or last movements of a composition. It is generally of an impromptu character.

Canon — A composition in which each voice imitates the preceding voice exactly.

Cantata — A work of several movements composed of arias, recitatives, and choruses.

Caprice (Fr.) or **Capriccio** (It.) — A whimsical, humorous composition.

Carol — A song of praise usually applied to songs sung at Christmas time.

Castanet — A pair of small pieces of hard wood used to accompany Spanish dancing.

Cello (It.) — An abbreviation of violoncello.

Chamber music — Compositions of instrumental music in the form of string quartets or quintets; pieces suitable for performance in an intimate setting.

Chanson (Fr.) — Song.

Chant — To recite musically.

Choral — Compositions for many voices; music composed for the chorus or choir.

Chord — Any combination of musical sounds.

Chord, common — A chord consisting of a fundamental note together with its third and fifth.

Chord, inverted — A chord whose notes are so arranged that the root does not appear as the lowest note.

Chromatic — 1) Proceeding by half steps; 2) any music or chord containing notes which do not belong to the diatonic scale.

Church modes — Plain-song or chant (see Gregorian chant).

Circle of fifths — A method of modulation, from dominant to dominant, which takes one through all the scales and back to the starting point.

Clarinet — A full-toned wind instrument often made of wood with a single-reed mouth piece.

Clavichord — A stringed instrument from the Middle Ages which is the forerunner of the harpsichord and piano.

Clavier (Ger.) — The German name for harpsichords, clavichords, and pianos.

Clef — The character used to determine the name and pitch of the notes on the staff.

Coda (It.) — The end.

Common time — A term sometimes used to refer to a piece of music with two beats in a bar or any multiple of two beats in a bar.

Con spirito (It.) — With spirit and energy.

Concert master — The chief violinist of an orchestra and the leader of the violins.

Concertina (It.) — A small instrument similar to the accordion with hexagonal sound boxes rather than oblong ones.

Concerto (It.) — A composition written to display a solo instrument, usually with orchestral accompaniment.

Conductor — The director or leader of an orchestra or chorus.

Console — The keyboard (including pedals and stops) of an organ.

Consonance — Sounds which, when played together, are agreeable to the ear.

Contralto (It.) — The lowest female voice (usually called alto).

Contrary motion — Melodic or harmonic motion in opposite directions.

Cornet — A brass instrument having valves or pistons. Similar to the trumpet.

Counterpoint — Point against point or melody against melody; the art of adding one or more additional melodies to a given melody.

Crescendo (It.) — Swelling or increasing the force of sound.

Cymbals — Circular brass plates which vibrate after being crashed together.

— D —

D — 1) The second note in the diatonic scale of C; 2) the key which has two sharps in its key signature.

D.C. — Da capo; from the beginning.

Da capo al fine (It.) — Return to the beginning and conclude at the word "fine."

Da capo al segno (It.) — Return to the beginning and play to the sign, after which play the coda.

Decrescendo (It.) — To gradually decrease in volume.

Diatonic — Proceeding in the order of the standard major or minor scale.

Diminished — Made less. Diminished intervals are those made less than minor.

Diminuendo (It.) — To become softer.

Discord — A combination of dissonant sounds.

Dissonance — A discord.

Dominant — The name applied to the fifth note of the scale.

Dominant chord — A chord built on the dominant or fifth note of the scale.

Dot — A dot under a note means that note should be played staccato. A dot after a note prolongs its time value by half.

Double bar — Two vertical lines drawn through the staff at the end of a section, movement, or the entire composition.

Double bass — The largest and lowest pitched instrument played with the bow.

Double flat — A character which lowers a tone two half steps.

Double reed — The mouthpiece of the oboe, bassoon, etc., formed by joining two pieces of cane together.

Double sharp — A character which raises a tone two half steps.

Double stopping — The stopping of two strings simultaneously with the fingers when playing the violin.

Double time — A time in which every measure is composed of two equal parts.

Duet — A composition for two voices or instruments.

Duple — Double; two beats in the measure.

Dynamics — Refers to expression in music (loudness and softness).

— E —

E — 1) In the scale of C, the third note; 2) the major key which has four sharps in its key signature.

Embellishment — The ornaments of melody, such as trills, turns, mordent, etc.

Embouchure (Fr.) — 1) The mouthpiece of a wind instrument; 2) the position of the mouth and lips of the player.

Enharmonic — Having intervals less than a semitone.

Etude (Fr.) — A study or exercise.

Expression — The act of rendering music so that it displays feelings and emotions.

— F —

F — 1) In the diatonic scale of C, the fourth note; 2) the name of the major scale which has one flat in its key signature.

f — The abbreviation of forte; ***ff***, fortissimo; ***fff***, fortississimo.

Falsetto (It.) — The artificial high tones of the voice.

Fanfare — A trumpet flourish or trumpet call.

Fermata (It.) — A hold.

Fife — A small shrill musical instrument of the flute type.

Fifth — An interval measuring five diatonic degrees. Also refers to the fifth degree in any diatonic scale.

Finale (It.) — The closing number of the last movement in a large musical composition.

Fine — The end.

Fingering — 1) The method of applying fingers to the keys, strings, or holes of various instruments; 2) the figures written on a page of music to show the performer which finger to use in playing a note.

Flat — The sign which lowers the pitch of the note one semi-tone.

Flute — A wind instrument of wood or metal, consisting of a tube closed at one end, with both holes and keys which are depressed or covered by the fingers.

Form — The melodic and rhythmic order in which musical ideas are presented.

Forte (It.) — Loudly.

Fortissimo (It.) — Extremely loud.

Fourth — An interval of four notes.

Frets — Small strips of wood, ivory, or metal placed upon the fingerboard of certain string instruments (i.e. guitars or banjos) to regulate the pitch of the notes produced.

Fugue — A polyphonic composition constructed on one or more short themes which are introduced from time to time with various contrapuntal devices.

Fundamental — The root on which any chord is built.

— G —

G — 1) The fifth note of the normal scale of C; 2) a keynote of a major scale which has one sharp in its key signature.

G clef — The treble clef.

Glissando (It.) — A flowing, unaccented execution of a passage or a rapid scale effect.

Glockenspiel (Ger.) — A set of small bars of polished steel which are struck with a mallet.

Grace note — An ornamental note or embellishment.

Grandioso (It.) — Grand, noble.

Grave (It.) — The slowest tempo in music.

Great octave — The notes lying between C and B inclusive.

Gregorian chant — A style of choral music introduced by Pope Gregory in the 6th century.

Ground bass — A constantly repeated bass passage of four or eight bars.

Guitar — A plucked stringed instrument of great resonance. The instrument is universally known and popular and has become a widely used solo instrument.

— H —

Half note — A note half the duration of a whole note.

Half rest — A rest half the duration of a whole rest.

Harmonic modulation — A change in the harmony from one key to another.

Harmonic scale — The scale formed by a series of natural harmonies.

Harmonica — A musical instrument which is also called a mouth organ.

Harmonics — Overtones.

73

Harmony — The art of combining tones into chords.

Harp — A stringed instrument of ancient origin, consisting of a triangular frame with strings which are played with the fingers.

Harpsichord — An instrument used extensively before the invention of the piano. The strings in a harpsichord are plucked by quills.

Hold — A character which indicates that a note or rest is to be prolonged (see **Fermata).**

Homophony — The opposite of polyphony; one melody supported by chords.

Horn — A metal wind instrument.

— I —

Improvisation — The art of singing or playing music without preparation.

Improvise — To create on the spur of the moment.

Incidental music — Descriptive music, generally orchestral, accompanying a play.

Instrument — Any mechanical contrivance for the production of musical sound.

Instrumentation — The art of using several musical instruments in combination.

In tempo — In strict time.

Interlude — A short piece played between longer musical sections or acts.

Intermezzo (It.) — A short piece or interlude.

Interval — The difference in pitch between two simultaneous tones.

Intonation — A word referring to the proper tonal emission, either vocal or instrumental.

Introduction — The preliminary movement of a composition which prepares the ear for the movements which are to follow.

Inversion — A change of position with respect to intervals and chords.

— J —

Jig — A lively dance.

Just — A term often applied to consonant intervals.

— K —

Kettle drum — An orchestral percussion instrument consisting of a hollow brass or copper shell over which a head is stretched.

Key — 1) A series of tones forming any given major or minor scale; 2) a finger or foot lever for producing tones on a piano or organ.

Keyboard — The whole series of levers for producing tones on a piano or organ.

— L —

Larghetto (It.) — Rather slow, but not as slow as largo.

Largo (It.) — Very slow.

Leading note — The seventh degree of an ascending scale.

Ledger lines — Short additional lines which are drawn above or below the staff.

Legato (It.) — In a smooth and connected manner.

Lento (It.) — Slow.

Libretto (It.) — The text of an opera or an oratorio.

Lute — An ancient stringed instrument; a predecessor of the guitar.

Lyre — One of the most ancient stringed instruments, similar to a harp.

— M —

mf — The abbrevation of mezzo forte.

M.M. — The abbreviation of Maelzel's Metronome.

mp — The abbrevation of mezzo piano.

Madrigal — An unaccompanied, polyphonic, secular composition.

Maestoso (It.) — Majestically and with dignity.

Major — Greater with respect to intervals and scales.

Major scale — The scale in which the half-steps fall between the third and fourth and the seventh and eighth tones both in ascending and descending order.

Mandolin — A pear-shaped instrument of the lute family with four strings.

Marcato (It.) — With marked emphasis.

March — A composition with strongly marked rhythm. It is generally written in 2/4 time.

Marimba — A percussion instrument made of a series of graduated pieces of hard wood which are struck with hammers.

Measure — The portion of the staff enclosed between two barlines.

Melody — A succession of tones rhythmically and symmetrically arranged to produce a pleasing effect.

Meno (It.) — Less.

Menuet (Fr.) — A slow dance in 3/4 time (a minuet).

Metronome — A mechanical device for determining the time value of the beat.

Mezzo (It.) — Half or medium.

Mezzo forte (It.) — Half loud.

Mezzo piano (It.) — Half soft.

Mezzo soprano (It.) — A voice lower in range than a soprano and higher than a contralto.

Middle C — The note which appears in the exact middle of the grand staff. It lies on the first ledger line above the bass staff and the first ledger line below the treble staff.

Minor (Lat.) — Less or smaller.

Minor scale — A scale formed by starting on the sixth degree of the major scale; also by lowering the third and sixth degrees of a given major scale one half step.

Mode — 1) A scale in Greek and early ecclesiastical music; 2) in modern usage, it is used with the terms major or minor, such as major mode or minor mode.

Moderato (It.) — Moderately.

Modulation — A change of key; the gradual movement from one key to another by a succession of chords.

Molto (It.) — Very much.

Monotone — To sing or recite words on a single note without changing pitch.

Mordent — A group of two or more grace notes played rapidly before a principle note.

Motet or **Motete** — A sacred composition for several voices.

Mouthpiece — The part of a wind instrument which is put into the mouth of the performer or against the performer's lips.

Movement — A division or portion of an extended composition.

Mute — 1) A small contrivance of wood or metal placed on the bridge of a stringed instrument to dampen the sound; 2) a pear-shaped contrivance placed in the bell of a brass instrument to dampen its sound.

— N —

Natural — A character used to cancel a sharp or a flat.

Neck — The part of stringed instruments such as violins or guitars which lies between the pegbox and the body of the instrument.

Neumes — Musical notation used in early Middle Ages; forerunner of notes.

Ninth — The interval of an octave plus a major or minor second.

Non troppo (It.) — Not too much.

Notation — The various signs used to represent music on the printed page, such as staves, clefs, notes, rests, etc.

Note — A printed sign which shows the relative duration and pitch of a sound.

— O —

Obligato — An additional part to a vocal or instrumental solo lying above the melody.

Oboe (It.) — A double-reed woodwind instrument.

Octave — Eight notes above or below a given note; the interval of an eighth.

Open strings — Strings which produce the sounds assigned to them on a particular instrument.

Opera — Musical drama; an extended musical work for voices and instruments which is produced with costumes, scenery, and dramatic effects.

Operetta — A little opera.

Opus (Lat.) — Work; used by composers to number their compositions.

Oratorio (It.) — A religious composition similar to an opera which is performed without costumes, scenery, or dramatic action.

Orchestra — A body of performers on string, woodwind, brass, and percussion instruments. The modern symphony orchestra consists of from 60 to 120 performers.

Orchestration — The art of composing or arranging music for an orchestra.

Overtones — Tones produced by a vibrating body above its fundamental tone.

Overture — An introductory selection, often a prelude to an opera or an oratorio.

— P —

p — Abbreviation used for the dynamic marking piano; *pp*, pianissimo.

Passage — 1) A musical phrase; 2) a musical figure.

Passing note — Notes which do not belong to the harmony.

Pedal — A mechanism controlled by the foot.

Pentatonic scale — The scale formed by the black keys of the piano.

Percussion — Any instrument that is struck (i.e. a drum, bell, cymbals, etc.).

Period — A complete musical sentence.

Phrase — Part of a musical sentence.

Phrasing — Dividing musical sentences into rhythmical sections.

Pianissimo (It.) — As softly as possible.

Piano (It.) — Softly.

Pianoforte (It.) — The complete name for a stringed instrument with a keyboard on which the tones are produced by felt hammers striking the strings.

Piccolo (It.) — 1) Small or little; 2) a small woodwind instrument similar to the flute.

Pitch — The height or depth of a tone.

Piu (It.) — More.

Pizzicato (It.) — The strings are to be plucked, which produces a staccato effect.

Plain chant or **Plain-song** — The names given to old ecclesiastical chants when they were in their most simple state and without harmony.

Plectrum (Lat.) — A quill used to pluck the strings on the harpsichord or other stringed instruments.

Poco (It.) — A little.

Poco a poco (It.) — Little by little.

Polonaise — A stately Polish dance in 3/4 time.

Polyphonic or **Polyphony** — Many-voiced; the blending of several independent melodies.

Portamento (It.) — Gliding from one note to another.

Prelude — A musical introduction to a composition.

Prestissimo (It.) — Very quickly.

Presto (It.) — Quickly; faster than allegro.

Primary accent — The accent beginning a measure.

Primary triad — One of the three fundamental triads of any key (I, IV, V).

Progression — The movement from note to note or from chord to chord.

— Q —

Quarter note — A note one-fourth the value of a whole note.

Quarter rest — A rest equal in time value to a quarter note.

Quartet — An instrumental or vocal composition for four performers.

Quintet — A composition for five solo performers.

— R —

Rallentando (It.) — Gradually slower.

Recitative — A type of musical declamation.

Reed — A thin strip of wood which, when vibrating, produces a musical sound.

Refrain — The chorus at the end of every verse of some songs.

Repeat — A sign which indicates that certain measures or passages are to be performed twice.

Rest — A sign which indicates silence of the same duration as the note for which it stands.

Rhythm — The division of musical ideas or sentences into regular metrical portions.

Rit. — Abbreviation of ritardando.

Ritardando (It.) — Retarding; delaying the time gradually.

Rondo (It.) — A composition which consists of a prominent theme alternating with other contrasting themes.

Root — The fundamental note of any chord.

Round — A form of canon in which several voices enter at staggered intervals but sing the same melody.

Rubato (It.) — Taking certain liberties with note duration. Some notes are held slightly longer and some notes are held slightly shorter than their exact values.

— S —

sf or *sfz* — Abbreviations for sforzando.

Saxophone — A metal woodwind instrument with a single-reed mouthpiece.

Scale — A series of consecutive tones proceeding by half steps (chromatic); half steps and whole steps (major); or by half steps and whole steps, with an occasional step and a half (minor).

Scherzo (It.) — Joke; a piece of music of a playful character.

Score — The whole instrumental or vocal parts of a composition written on separate staves and placed under each other.

Second — An interval measuring two diatonic degrees.

Secondary chords — Chords built on II, III, VI, or VII.

Section — A complete but not an independent musical idea. Also refers to a family of instruments within the orchestra.

Segno (It.) — A sign. Directs the performer to turn back and repeat from the place marked by the sign.

Segue (It.) — In a similar manner; go on.

Sempre (It.) — Always or continually.

Septet — A composition for seven voices or instruments.

Septuplet — A group of seven equal notes to be performed in the same time of four or six.

Sequence — The recurrence of a melodic motif.

Seventh — An interval measuring seven diatonic degrees.

Seventh chord — A chord composed of a root, its third, fifth, and seventh.

Sextet — A composition for six voices or instruments.

Sextuplet (Lat.) — A group of six notes to be played in the time of four.

Sforzando (It.) — With sudden emphasis.

Sharp — The sign which raises the pitch of a note one half step.

Sign — A note or character employed in printed music.

Signature — The signs, such as sharps, flats, or fractional figures, placed at the beginning of a piece of music.

Sixteenth note — A note one half the length of an eighth note.

Sixteenth rest — A pause equal in duration to a sixteenth note.

Sixth — An interval measuring six diatonic degrees.

Slide — 1) A movable tube in the trombone; 2) to pass from one note to another without any cessation of sound.

Slur — A curved line placed over notes directing that they be played legato.

Solo (It.) — Alone.

Sonata (It.) — An extended piano composition with several movements.

Soprano (It.) — The highest kind of female voice.

Sostenuto (It.) — Sustaining the tone.

Sotto voce (It.) — Softly, as in an undertone.

Space — On the staff, the interval between the lines or the ledger lines.

Staccato (It.) — In a crisp and detached manner.

Staff or **Stave** — The five parallel lines used in modern musical notation.

Stem — The line attached to a note head.

Step — A melodic progression of a second.

String quartet — A composition in four parts for two violins, viola, and cello.

Sub (Lat.) — Under or below.

Subdominant — The fourth degree of a scale.

Subito (It.) — Suddenly; at once.

Subject — A melody or theme.

Supertonic — The second degree of the scale.

Suspension — The holding or prolonging of a note in any chord into the chord which follows.

Sustained note — A name given to a prolonged note.

Symphonic poem — A form of orchestral composition originated by Liszt.

Symphony — A large composition of several movements for a full orchestra. Also, often used to refer to the orchestra itself.

Syncopation — The shifting of an accent from a strong beat to a weak beat.

— T —

Tablature (Fr.) — A system of notation used for fretted instruments such as guitar and banjo.

Tempo (It.) — Rate of movement or speed.

Tempo mark — A word or phrase indicating the rate of speed of a piece of music.

Tenor — The highest male voice.

Tenor clef — The C clef on the fourth line.

Tenuto (It.) — Held or sustained.

Ternary — Progressing by threes.

Tessitura (It.) — The range from lowest to highest tone.

Tetrachord — A series of four consecutive notes.

Theme — 1) The subject of a fugue; 2) simple melody on which variations are made.

Thorough bass — Basso continuo; a system of harmony developed in the 1600's which is indicated by a figured bass.

Tie — A curved line joining two notes of the same pitch and adding the duration of the second note to the first.

Time — The division of musical phrases into portions marked by a regular accent.

Tonality — Pertaining to the key.

Tone — 1) Sound; 2) often refers to a Gregorian chant.

Tonic — The keynote of a scale.

Tonic chord — The common chord of which the tonic is the root.

Transition — Modulation; a passing note.

Transpose — To perform or write out a composition in a different key.

Transposing instruments — Musical instruments which are in any key other than C. The actual sound or key produced depends upon the instrument itself.

Treble — The highest voice or part; also refers to the G clef.

Tremolo (It.) — A quivering or fluttering.

Triad — A chord of three notes.

Triangle — A percussion instrument made of a steel rod bent into a three-sided shape and struck with a small metal bar.

Trill (Fr.) — A shake, usually produced by the rapid alternation of two notes.

Trio (It.) — 1) A piece for three voices; 2) a section of a minuet, march, etc.

Triplet — A group of three notes performed in the time of two.

Trombone — A brass wind instrument which consists of two tubes sliding in and out of each other.

Trumpet — A brass wind instrument with valves.

Tuba — A valved brass instrument of very low pitch.

Tune — 1) A simple melody; 2) intonation.

Tuning — The adjustment of an instrument to a recognized pitch.

Turn — An embellishment consisting of a group of rapid notes connecting one principle note with another.

Tutti (It.) — Everyone.

— U —

Unison — Singing exactly the same note, or an octave for mixed voices or instruments.

Un poco (It.) — A little.

Upbeat — An unaccented beat.

— V —

Valse (Fr.) — Waltz.

Valve — In brass instruments, a device which shortens or lengthens the brass tubing to sound the semitones and tones between the natural open harmonies.

Variation — Certain modifications with regard to the time, tune, and harmony of a theme.

Vibrato (It.) — A tremulous quality of tone.

Viol — An instrument similar to the violin, but a little larger and with six strings.

Viola (It.) — An orchestral stringed instrument similar to the violin, but larger. Music for this instrument is written in the alto clef.

Violin — The leading stringed instrument in the orchestra, composed of a gracefully shaped wooden box with four strings. It is most often played by means of a bow.

Violoncello (It.) — A four-stringed, bowed instrument shaped like a violin, but held between the knees while playing.

Virtuoso (It.) — A great instrumental or vocal artist.

Vivace (It.) — Very lively.

Vocal — Music intended to be sung.

Voice — The sounds produced by the human organs of speech. Also may be used to refer to one of the parts in a polyphonic composition.

Volume — A term which refers to the power and quality of the tone.

— W —

Waltz — A dance with three beats to the measure. Classical waltzes are compositions in waltz form, but are intended for performance.

Whole note — The longest note in value used in modern notation.

Whole rest — A pause equal in length to a whole note.

Whole step — A major second.

Whole-tone scale — A series of six consecutive whole steps.

Wind instrument — Any musical instrument whose sound is produced by the player's breath or by means of some type of bellows.

Woodwind — The orchestral family of instruments composed of flutes, oboes, clarinets, bassoons, and similar instruments.

— XYZ —

Xylophone — A percussion instrument which dates to very early times, consisting of wooden bars tuned to the tones of the scale and struck with mallets.

Zither (Ger.) — A flat stringed instrument consisting of a shallow wooden sound box.

Other Helpful Resources from Mel Bay Publications

Carlton's Complete Musical Dictionary & Encyclopedia

Student's Guide to the Great Composers

Student's Guide to Music Theory

Student's Musical Dictionary

Theory & Harmony for Everyone

You Can Teach Yourself About Music